C000178342

6
Questions

Six Questions

Peter Freeth

Published by

Communications In Action

2008

Six Questions

First Edition – July 2005
Reprinted November 2004
Second Edition July 2008

ISBN 0-954-57481-8
ISBN 978-0-954-57481-9

Communications In Action 2008

© Peter Freeth 2000 to 2008

Peter Freeth has asserted his rights under the Copyright, Designs and Patents act 1988 to be identified as the author of this work.

All rights reserved in all media. This book may not be copied, stored, transmitted or reproduced in any format or medium without specific prior permission from Peter Freeth. Contact Peter Freeth for information about multiple licenses, library copies and review copies.

Published by:

Communications In Action
49 Fishponds Road
Kenilworth
Warwickshire
CV8 1EY
United Kingdom

www.ciauk.com   0870 1620802
peter@ciauk.com   +44 870 1620802

Six Questions

Introduction

Problems are a part of daily life. Many people and organisations seem afraid to use the word these days, instead talking about "issues" or "challenges". This half-hearted attempt to reframe problems as opportunities does not convince most people who still need practical help in solving those daily blocks and dilemmas.

The great news for problem solvers everywhere is that much bigger problems than yours have been solved during the course of human history. The size of a problem is mostly down to perception and being closer to it certainly does make it seem bigger. If a problem is on top of you, you cannot see clearly around or over it.

Many people concentrate their effort on the problem, possibly thinking that familiarity with it will generate a solution. This is almost never the case. Concentrating your attention on the problem will only make it bigger, because you get more of what you focus on. The first priority in problem solving is to attend to the desired outcome. It's no use worrying about what you haven't got – it's what you want that is important.

Here's a demonstration for you. Call a local decorator and ask him to paint your bedroom "not blue". Then get into a long and painful discussion that centres around every colour he suggests being wrong. Then finally settle on a colour that he calls "blue" and that you call "turquoise" or "lilac".

Perhaps this sounds like a familiar routine for some of the problems you have had in the past? Certainly, using vague language like "blue" or "professional" or "truth" gives rise to many unnecessary problems. It does seem that we are divided by a common language.

This book is about easily solving day to day problems by changing the way that people think, and in order to achieve this, we have some simple principles to work with, such as:

- ▫ Concentrate on what you do want instead of what you don't want

- ▫ Stop looking for solutions

- ▫ If you don't yet have the resources you need to solve the problem, borrow them

- ▫ Fight the urge to look for reasons – they are irrelevant

- ▫ Ask "do we need this problem?"

- ▫ Ask "are we doing this because it's the right thing to do, or are we doing it because we're doing it?"

Some of these principles may make sense straightaway. Others may be counter-intuitive. Certainly, in a world of law suits, public enquiries and management consultancies, you could be forgiven for thinking that knowing why a problem exists is important. This information is important if you want to study the problem for intellectual or historical reasons. This information is important if the problem is mechanical or procedural in nature and you want to prevent the exact same problem from arising in the future. This information is not important if you just want to solve a business or personal problem and move on.

No two problems involving human beings can ever be the same, because people will evolve and change and will have different experiences to draw upon in each situation. Therefore, finding out "why?" something went wrong last time is of no value at all, because next time, everything will be different.

This handbook is a practical guide to creative problem solving. Reading this book is an invitation to cast aside the ways that you used to tackle problems. After all, if you could solve every problem you had easily, you wouldn't be reading this!

There are three important points here that you can bear in mind as you are reading. The first is that this is a practical book - there is no theory here, only practice. These tools work, not because of any clever trick or script but because they change the way that people think. The tools here only work when you use them. Just thinking about using them won't make any difference to your problems.

The second point is that this approach to solving problems is creative. Creativity has a special meaning here - it means that you are invited to abandon the way you used to approach problems. Those old ways don't work - that's why you need to find new ways. You may have heard before that if what you're doing isn't working, do something different. The difficulty is finding new ways to think - and this book can help you.

Creativity means to detach from a solution, a right answer or a perfect outcome. To be looking for a right answer means that you already know how the answer should be, and that is part of the problem because it's part of the way you're thinking about the problem. Creative problem solvers don't look for solutions, they generate lots of ideas. If one of those ideas becomes a solution then that's a bonus, but it cannot be your objective.

Humans, as a species, are successful because we have innate creative abilities. We can create solutions to problems that are different to a simple linear extension of the problem. We can create solutions that are unique, innovative, or that use existing materials and resources in a new way. When you're at your intellectual peak, you have access to these capabilities. When stuck inside a problem, people often revert to linear thinking that generates solutions like "try harder" or "work faster". The basic creative solution that you will generate with the help of this book is "do something different".

There's nothing wrong with being stuck - we all get stuck when our thinking is constrained by a problem. When our minds are caged in this way, it doesn't matter how hard and long you think, because your intellectual capacity is limited by the problem itself. What you need at this point is something to help you break outside of those boundaries.

Finally, this book is a guide, not a set of rules. Take what you can learn here, add it to your own experience and create new ideas, new tools and new solutions to old problems.

Most of all, enjoy the results you will get. Stop taking problems so seriously and treat them for what they are. Just problems.

Why?

"Why?" is a great question to use when you want to get a list of reasons, justifications and rational explanations relating to the existence of a problem.

Did you know that we all have a critical filter?

Critical Filter

The filter protects you from other people's commands and beliefs. If someone says you have to do something, you can stop and think about what's in it for you. If they say something is true, you can stop and think about whether it is true for you or not.

Imagine that a meeting goes badly and a colleague says to you, "It was great, really!" and you answer, "Yes, I suppose so". On the inside, you know that the meeting really did go badly.

When you have a problem, how do you respond to helpful friends who give you advice in the form, "I'll tell you what you need to do..."?

This direct form of communication simply bounces harmlessly off your critical filter so there's no chance of it pulling you off course.

Your expectations, experience and goals program the filter so that you only hear what you want to hear. When you are convinced that your idea is brilliant, you might not hear criticism, and when you are convinced things are going badly, no-one can convince you otherwise.

Fortunately, there are ways that we can communicate through this critical filter.

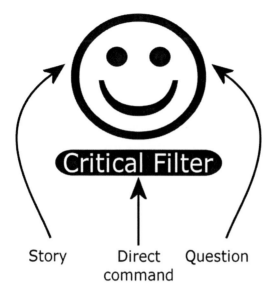

Story   Direct   Question
command

Stories bypass the critical filter because they're not true and they're not about you, so there's no need to worry.

Questions bypass the critical filter because they instantly put the listener into a receptive state. Don't take my word for this; try it for yourself.

Next time you are in a meeting and you want to ask a question, say this:

"Can I ask you a question?"

And before you carry on, notice what happens. You will be amazed to see many people stop what they're doing and look up, giving you their full attention.

Of course, questions don't only request information – they can carry a hidden payload of information too. Questions are therefore amongst the most powerful influence tools that you have at your disposal.

One of the problems with the question "why?", however, is that it often causes the critical filter to become even more sensitive. Many people regard "why?" as questioning their judgement, and in effect, it is. "Why?" asks someone to give their reasoning, which is part of their judgement, so some people respond to this question by becoming rather defensive.

The question "why?" also serves a very useful secondary purpose. When you ask someone "why", their own answer will convince them even more that their problem is unsolvable. A particularly powerful version of a "why?" question is the form "why not?" or "why don't you?"

When you ask why something is not happening, you will hear in response a list of logical and plausible reasons that prove that the thing cannot be done or that the problem cannot be solved. From the person's limited view of the world, they are right - they cannot see how the problem can be solved because their thinking is constrained by the history of the problem itself.

"Why?" is the perfect question to ask when you want to deeply embed a person into their own self imposed set of rules, because the answer can only be created from their interpretation of how things happen in the world. Their rules about right and wrong and cause and effect constrain the answer that they will give you.

Usually, you will have very good intentions when you ask the question "why?" You may want to learn what has caused something to happen, or you may want to learn how someone makes decisions. You might also want to motivate someone or guide them by asking "why don't you…..?" Just bear in mind for a moment the idea that cause and effect is an illusion created by your brain as one of the many defence mechanisms we have evolved as a species.

The question "why?" focuses attention on the problem or limitation, thereby making it bigger, clearer and more real.

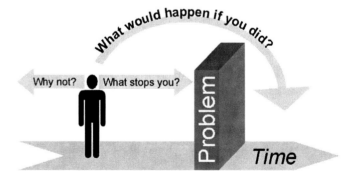

Why are you reading this? Why aren't you working instead? Why can't you get over that problem? Why did you make that decision?

Was that helpful to you? Try this instead:

How did you decide to read this? What would you achieve if you were working instead? What stops you from getting over that problem? How were you able to make that decision?

These questions are asking for the same information, but they are causing your brain to recover that information differently. It's no accident that there are different words that seem on the face of it to imply the same meaning. Pick up any thesaurus and look up a list of synonyms of a word and think whether their meaning is exactly the same. Think about each word by imagining what it means to you in terms of a sensory experience - what you can see, hear, feel, taste and smell. Here's an example:

Professional - Expert - Proficient - Specialist

In order for your brain to recover the meaning of these words, you recover some specific experiences from your past that match the label of the word. If you thought of your brain as a filing room, what files would be in the drawer marked "professional" and how would these differ from those in the drawer marked "expert"?

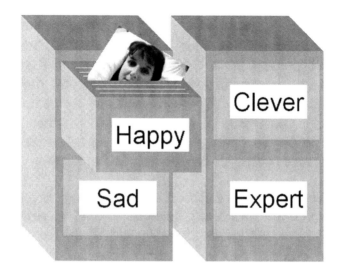

It's the same with any language, because language is only a pale, hollow representation of the rich sensory experience that is in your head. When you use language to communicate with another person, you are inviting them to recover files from their own filing room and use them to construct the meaning of what you say. It's no wonder that communication sometimes doesn't have the effect we expect or intend.

The process by which we recover a sensory experience from language is, of course, unconscious and practically instantaneous. By the time you become aware of something, it has already happened, so it's even faster than instantaneous!

An interesting process that often creates the rules that we hear in response to the question "why?" is cause and effect. An event occurs, time elapses and then a second event occurs. Which events do we choose to connect with the word "because"? The answer lies in the rules that govern our experience and our interaction with the world. We connect the two events together as if they are related, so when one happens again, we expect the other to happen.

We could not function without rules, as we would be unable to formulate useful theories and generalisations about the world we live in. In order to survive, we must know in advance that lions and cars are dangerous and that bread and water are safe. Since we are unable to know in advance what the future holds, we must be able to predict as accurately as possible what is likely to happen. As children, we experiment ruthlessly and continually. We sit on broken chairs, balance on precarious ledges, put all manner of things in our mouths and watch other people like hawks. The next time you see a young child, notice how they watch other people. Notice where they look. Notice how their facial expressions change with the fleeting moods of the person under inspection.

Therefore, we begin to generalise cause and effect in the world and in our interaction with it. If we drop different objects and they all move towards the floor, we can assume that there is some force that pulls objects downwards. Have you seen a child with their first balloon? Why do they let go? In order to test this interesting new violation of the gravity rule, the child must let go of the balloon and away it floats...

Often, people will use the word "because" as part of the language pattern "conclusion because evidence". If we were to take this pattern literally and express it as a cause and effect sequence, it becomes "evidence leads to conclusion" which is, of course, obvious.

Another way of expressing this "because" structure is "meaning because experience". In other words, a person generalises a meaning or inference from a set of data gathered either from external sensory stimulus or from internal memory. That internal memory is itself a generalised, distorted version of past events.

In 'real time', events happen, then we experience them, then we think about them, then we create meaning from them:

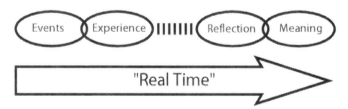

All of this takes time. It might take only a few seconds, or it might take minutes, hours, days, weeks, months or years. We can continue to look back on past experiences and make new meaning from them, and when we do that, we reverse the flow of time:

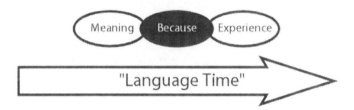

"I'll never be successful here because of the way they treated me..." is an example I hear. The sequence of time runs backwards, and the word "because" also creates future connections and future examples of the problem.

Remember, when a person tells you about a problem, they're not really telling you about a problem. They're telling you about an example of the problem. The problem is the underlying set of perceptions, beliefs and processes which turn a sensory experience into something that can be labelled as a "problem".

What is important here is that you treat the word "because" as an indication of the operation of rules rather than as a justification of a fact or sequence of events.

Here are some examples.

Typical "Because" version

Useful cause and effect version

I won't be promoted because I don't have the experience

In the past, I have seen someone promoted and guessed the reason why. This reason does not apply to me, so I will choose not to be promoted.

We can't make changes because the boss won't like it

In the past, the boss has appeared to dislike something. During constant change, I have noticed differences in specific areas that I have associated with the boss's reaction. I am now imagining that my colleagues feel the same way. Therefore, we are not able to suggest changes.

My project will fail because I don't have the right staff

My staff bear some resemblance to people I worked with in the past when a project did not turn out as I had imagined it would. I can't see any mistake on my part. I have decided that my project will fail.

In any of these examples, what is important is that you recognise the special significance of because, cause and effect and the rules that allow us to predict future behaviour from past experience. For objects without free will, we can only predict behaviour when we understand universal governing laws. For example, when you drop a ball you can predict that it will fall because you know about gravity. We learn about these physical laws intuitively, without needing physics teachers to give us names for them.

You intuitively know how much hot and cold water to put in the bath without needing to know about its specific latent heat of evaporation. You know how to balance a stack of building blocks without having to know about centres of gravity. As a child, you could throw and catch a ball long before you learned about Newton's laws of motion. We are born experimenters. The problem is that we use our innate ability to generalise physical laws to create laws for the behaviour of people and animals.

You might hear people on the news say that their dog would never hurt a fly, just after it has attacked a child. You often hear the neighbours of serial killers say that the killer was very quiet and polite and they couldn't imagine him doing anything like that. On the other hand, you might cross the road when you see a group of noisy teenagers and judge people by the colour of their skin.

We unwittingly use our ability to predict future events to predict the behaviour of people based only on what we can observe directly. There's nothing wrong with this - it's a very useful skill - just be careful how you use it!

This next paragraph is very important, so read it carefully and take as long as you need to decide its relevance to you.

Experience is of little use to you since it relates to events that happened in the past, somewhere else and with different people. Any similarity to current events is a trick played on you by your brain, which is trying to avoid hard work by simplifying what it tells you about the world.

Essentially, our ability to notice patterns and infer cause and effective relationships only works well for inanimate objects. For anything with a mind of its own, these rules no longer work well enough to be useful.

Rationally, you know that things that have happened in the past do not automatically recur in the future without some intervention. Buses and trains run every day of the working week, yet they will not continue to run without their drivers consciously intervening. When the bus doesn't turn up, we get impatient and say "it *should* be here by now". We feel put out when things don't happen as we expect. The sun came up yesterday so we're confident that the sun will come up tomorrow. The coffee machine worked yesterday so we expect it to work tomorrow. There's nothing wrong with this - in fact, this expectation has probably saved your life a few times. If crossing the road was dangerous yesterday, it's probably still dangerous tomorrow. It's just important to notice when this expectation serves a useful purpose for you and when it doesn't.

It is very important that I point out the key to this approach - it's effective with the kinds of problems that we make for ourselves. If your problem is connected with mechanical failure or some other physical event, then this book will still help you to think creatively about a solution. For the most part, however, this book will help you to unblock problems that have been created by humans, for example "we couldn't launch a product like that", or "I could never learn to do that" or even "there's no point me applying for that job - I won't get it"

Always keep in mind that when you ask "why?", you don't get reasons – you get reasoning. And that is completely different.

Here's another thought about the word "because" - that hearing someone else state their reason for doing a certain thing gives you absolutely zero useful information. I hear many people say "but if I knew their reasons then at least I could understand", and to this I say two things. Firstly, hearing the words they use to rationalise an instinctive choice is not the same as knowing their reason. Secondly, you can understand without having to know their reasons, and here's how. Whenever you feel tempted to ask "why?" then just rest assured the answer is "just because".

Many years ago, some friends and I visited Amsterdam for a weekend. Amongst the other cultural delights that the city has to offer, we visited a diamond factory. Of course, they don't make diamonds there, I just don't know the proper name for the place. The owner was giving us a tour and he told us that there are two types of diamond - the clear (white) ones we're familiar with, and black ones. One of my friends asked "Why are the black diamonds black?" and the owner replied "because they are not white".

As you can see, the answer makes perfect sense - it's the question that's meaningless. Why is this book a book? Because it's not a teapot. Why did you make that decision? Because I didn't make a different one. Why am I telling you all this? Because I am. So there.

Cause and effect is the result of our brains connecting together events which happened at different times. Your breakfast doesn't cause your lunch, sunrise doesn't cause the hands on your watch to move and other people don't cause you to feel a certain way.

Of course, since people are wired up to relate cause and effect, you can use this knowledge to influence people. If you say "I need to push in front of you because I'm late for work" then some people will let you in. Oddly enough, if you say "I need to push in because I have a tomato in my pocket" then those same people will still let you in. Try it for yourself and see. There's a much longer explanation of this in Robert Cialdini's excellent "Influence: Science and Practice".

This is also important when you're reinforcing beliefs and behaviours that are useful, so for example if someone says, "I want to go to the gym more often", then asking "why?" results in a stronger commitment. Just always bear in mind that there is an implicit agreement in "why?" which will reinforce the preceding belief.

So, our remarkable human ability to learn from past experiences helps us to survive, but it also causes some problems too when it is left unchecked. Just don't confuse "past experiences" with "experience". Whenever you want to be truly creative, leave past experiences where they belong - in the past.

Asking "Why?" gets people to make connections between events - connections that they may have not made before, but now those connections seem very reasonable indeed. Before you know it, the problem becomes true and immovable. Once again, you may want to achieve this so I won't say "Never ask why" - instead I'll say "Be careful when you ask why".

Everyone with a problem is an excellent hypnotist, because they can draw you into their world through their stories which seem so convincing and so seductive. Just remember that their stories and reasons make sense simply because they are grammatically correct. They are neither true nor false, they are only part of the story teller's current reality, and since that reality defines the problem, it may not be the best place to look for a solution.

Since you know this rationally, why can't you stop thinking that past failures mean the same outcome for similar future activities? Because you have rules that are no longer useful to you, that's why.

It's time to break those rules.

How?

How do you know that you have this problem?

Well, that sounds like an odd question, until you really start to think about it. How do you know? What evidence have you collected to support your belief that you have this problem?

Most importantly, what sensory evidence have you collected? What have you seen, heard and felt that lets you know you have this problem?

How will you know that this problem is solved? How will you test that the solution is what you wanted? If you don't know what you want, how will you know when you have it?

Over time, problems become embedded in our beliefs. Our problems become "true" and the only variable is "how hard do I need to try to solve this problem?" Sometimes, you end up with problems you don't need just because you've gotten used to them. Well, it's time to forget about them, leave them all behind and move onto more important problems. If you've got a problem which is just lingering, get rid of it!

But how?

As you read through this book, you may have missed the importance of that first question, so here it is again:

How do you know that you have this problem?

The problem manifests itself in your mind as a collection of sensory stimuli. How is an intangible problem built and maintained inside your mind? How do you carry this problem around with you when you're away from the direct environment of the problem? If you take your work problems home with you, or if you take your home problems to work with you, how do you carry them around?

If you've ever stewed in a problem, long after the actual situation has gone away, then you have carried round a representation of the problem with you. You have not carried an exact replica of the problem - you have filtered and squashed and converted the problem into a format that suits your state of mind. How did you do this? More importantly, how can you use this knowledge to pull the problem apart? After all, if the situation has passed, why do you still need the problem?

In the film Get Shorty, Rene Russo asks John Travolta if he was scared during a fight. He tells her that he was and she says that he isn't acting like he's scared. His reply sums this idea up perfectly..."I was scared then, not now. How long do you want me to be scared?"

You may also want to consider how the problem works, how it exists as a problem. Remember that this thing exists as a problem because you have constructed it that way. This problem does not exist outside of you. How do I know this? Because you can't put the problem in a wheelbarrow. Whilst parts of this problem may be common to a number of people, the problem has a different meaning to each of you. Your specific version of the problem therefore exists only within you.

Remember, the "problem" that you talk about is not one problem. Each person you talk to will have a different representation of it - they will each carry around a different collection of thoughts and memories that represent the problem, so it's very important to get these representations out in the open, rather than assume that everyone has the same problem. One of the easiest and quickest ways to do this is to ask "what is this problem like?" so that you get a metaphor for the problem from each person involved. You'll be surprised at the range of answers you get, and they will give you a much more accurate understanding of the problem than a direct description of the problem itself.

Metaphor is a very powerful tool for breaking down complex problems because it bypasses people's conscious beliefs and preconceptions about what they should say and what they think the solution is. Metaphors are also important because they convey far more information than a logical description, and they convey information that resides at the unconscious level.

You may think it sounds a little strange to ask someone how they know they have a problem, so try it for yourself and find out what happens. As human beings, we respond not to direct sensory experience but to meaning - our sensory experience, distorted by our beliefs and expectations and converted into meaning.

For example, let's say that you're annoyed at someone because of what they have done. The problem is not their behaviour – the problem is how you feel about it. How can I say this? Easily, and for two reasons. Firstly, their behaviour is not under your control so it's not your problem. Secondly, their behaviour is in the past so you cannot change it, whereas you can easily change how you feel about it as that is in the present.

You will see this happening all around you, every day, when you pay attention to the events that make people respond emotionally. When a friend doesn't call, it's because they're avoiding you. When a customer doesn't call, it's because they don't like you. When your child doesn't call, something has happened to them.

In all of these examples, your emotional response and your behaviour are driven not by the raw information (the telephone is not ringing) but by the meaning you attach to this information.

Often, the meaning that we attach is a useful one and it helps us to take action that is appropriate to our chosen outcome. Often, the meaning is not useful. Spending a day worrying about the call you haven't had from a client doesn't help you.

Does this make a real difference? Let's take a real example and find out. I recently worked with a recruitment consultant who was expecting a call from a candidate to accept a job offer. The candidate hadn't called, hadn't responded to several messages and his mobile telephone was switched off. The consultant spent the whole morning running through what was happening. He convinced himself that the candidate was avoiding him and that he was going to turn down the job offer. I managed to persuade the consultant that all that had happened so far was that the candidate hadn't called. Perhaps he had had an accident? Perhaps he had gone away with his family? Perhaps he just wanted some peace and quiet to get himself prepared to hand in his notice?

By focussing on the reality of the situation, the consultant calmed down considerably and was able to focus on something much more important at that time - preparing himself for an important client meeting later that day.

That evening, the candidate called to accept the offer. The consultant answered the call by saying something like "It's nice to hear from you, I was a little worried" and the candidate said he'd just gone out for the day and his mobile had a flat battery. Now, that may or may not be true but that's not important. What's important is that the candidate did call and did accept the job and there was no point worrying about it whilst there were many more important things to think about.

In most cases - average cases - this won't make a big difference. Imagine the case where the candidate is truly undecided and, based on the call to the consultant could decide one way or the other. Now imagine a consultant who is convinced the candidate will turn down the offer. When the consultant answers the phone and says "Oh, it's you. I take it you're turning down the offer?" the candidate picks up his doubt and uncertainty and the decision will be more likely to go unfavourably for the consultant. Whether we like it or not, we influence people all day long, not just with the words we use but more powerfully with our tone of voice and facial expression. In average, day to day situations, there's a wide enough margin for error that you could do pretty much anything and get away with it. In situations where the outcome is less certain, or there's more at stake, you need to be in a positive, resourceful state that will infect other people and make these situations more likely to develop in your favour.

So, the simple question was "how do you know the candidate is avoiding calling you?" and the answer was that, really, he didn't. Now in this case, that turned out to be wrong. At other times, it will be right, but there's still nothing to gain in dwelling on it and worrying about it. It's still more useful to focus on something more productive. In fact, if the consultant had been right about the candidate, wouldn't it have been even more important to be in the most resourceful state for that client meeting, so that the consultant could win at least some business back?

So, how you're going to work on the problem is a very important thing to think about.

What?

"What?" identifies the nature of the problem. What is it? What do we know about it? What shall we call it? What are you doing about it?

Applying the question "what?" to the problem itself may help clarify it, but aside from that it's not much use. Here are some questions that are far more useful in solving the problem.

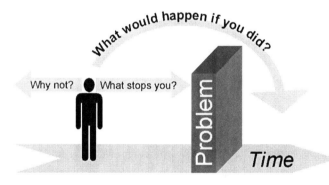

In the "Why?" chapter, we talked about the effect of asking "Why?" or "Why not?" in directing your attention to the past where events cannot be changed. You'll have noticed two other questions in the diagram that I can now tell you more about.

What stops you?

This question focuses your attention on the barrier – the problem as it exists in the future and which stops you from taking action to achieve what you want. Since the barrier is in the future, it doesn't really exist. For example, I couldn't be an author because no-one will buy my books. You may have wished you hadn't bought my book, but the fact remains that you did. Therefore the barrier only exists in my mind since everything in the future exists only in our minds!

So, I can imagine a barrier in the future and it prevents me from taking action now. Isn't it better that I take action now and not worry about what may or may not happen in the future? Of course it is – so why does it still happen?

You might hear people say things like "I won't apply for that job because I won't get it" or "I won't ask that girl out because she will say no" or even "I won't present because the audience will doubt my credibility".

None of those statements are true in any sense of shared reality, but they are true in that they paralyse people and prevent them from exploring their own potential.

By focussing on that barrier, at least we can learn more about it and discover ways to move past it.

Do you ever worry? Worry is simply a process of imagining something that you don't want to happen, which of course makes it more likely to happen.

When you find yourself influencing other people with your worries, take a moment to ask yourself, "what do I imagine is going to happen?" and then change the picture to something more useful.

For example, let's say you're worried about a particular project going badly, so you help the people involved in it to do a good job by reminding them, "don't forget to check the pricing" or, "don't put that there" or even, "make sure we don't lose this deal". It's far more useful to say, "check the pricing", "put that there instead" or even, "what else do we need to do to win this deal?"

Here's an example of a typical interaction using this approach, remembering that worry is simply hijacking your natural goal setting software, so the more you worry, the better you are at setting goals. This example is from a presentation skills workshop.

Pete:	What do you imagine is going to happen?
Miss X:	I'll be nervous and won't be able to breathe
Pete:	Is that what you want to happen?
Miss X:	No!
Pete:	What do you want to happen?
Miss X:	I want to feel relaxed and enjoy myself
Pete:	And what happens when you imagine that?
Miss X:	It's great!
Pete:	Well imagine that then!

What would happen if you did?

What would happen if you did apply for the job? What would happen if you did ask her out? What would happen if you did present to that audience?

In order to process the language of this question, you have to create an internal representation of a solution. As soon as you do that, the solution becomes possible, even though you don't yet know what the solution is in detail. The questions in this book are not intended as a magic wand to magically banish problems – each one will shake the problem loose a little so that you can solve it yourself – once you know that it can be solved.

What if?

"What if?" is a nice question to ask if your intention is to generate possibilities. Be careful not to guide the problem onto a new track, as your purpose is to free the problem of its cage and let it generate new solutions. If you only ask "What if we did this instead?" then you may be in danger of pushing the problem down a new alleyway.

You could successfully use this question to explore the implications or consequences of a problem by asking "What if this happened?" or "What if we all went home and slept on it?"

By the way, when you make a major decision like which car or house to buy or who to marry, there's no way that most people would let themselves be pushed into deciding straight away without giving themselves time to think. Since dreaming is an excellent way of organising and sorting new information, sleeping on a problem or decision is a very effective way of gaining new insight into it.

In business, people are often pressured into making hasty decisions. For example, a team will need to reach a decision before they go home from the office. Why? If it's important enough, sleep on it.

What would it be like?

Now we are entering the realm of guiding other people's thoughts in a new direction. What would it be like if, as you are reading these words, you start to imagine yourself in the future, having long since forgotten about those old problems. If you were in this present situation again at some future point in time, armed with all of your experience and knowledge, how would you solve the problem more easily?

You'll notice there were a few questions in there, but the one that started the process was "What would it be like?". When you ask someone this question, they can suspend disbelief, put their worries and issues to one side and let themselves enter a daydream that you will now guide them through. You don't need to prescribe the steps needed to solve the problem - you only need to help them experience how nice it will feel to have solved it.

What else?

It seems such an obvious thing to say, yet many people aren't able to access the simple understanding of "if what you are doing isn't working, do something else".

Problems create a problem state - a problem mindset. When all of your thoughts become constrained by the problem, it can be very difficult to think about what else you could do differently to get better results. Even looking for a solution means that your thinking is constrained by the problem, which is why it's important to detach from that outcome and instead seek ideas and possibilities.

This is probably not the best question to start with, but would be a very useful question to open up a mind that was just beginning to think past the problem. You could ask "What else would work?" or "What else do you need to learn in order to solve this problem?"

What would it take?

Sometimes, solutions have a price. A problem creates a certain environment which some people can comfortably reside in for a long, long time. In other words, some people have really useful problems.

What would it take for you to give up the positive aspects of the problem in order to solve it? Of course, this presumes that problems have positive aspects and in fact they often do, so it's really important that you don't throw the baby out with the bathwater when you solve a problem. You may find that a problem gives you motivation or gains you the attention of others. In this case, you need to find another way to get what you need. The "What else?" question would be really helpful in this case.

The important point for this particular question is "What would it take for you to solve this problem?"

This question has a very useful side effect in that it also points attention towards the resources that may be needed in order to generate a good outcome.

What next?

Don't just sit there! Do something!

The question is "what?" It sometimes seems important, especially with organisational problems, to have a fully formed, complicated plan of action that sets out specific procedural actions on behalf of various people.

Resist this temptation. It's irrelevant. You do not yet have enough information to see that far ahead into the resolution stage.

The only information you need as you enter the resolution stage is "What shall I do first?"

As you start to move out of the problem state and start thinking about resolutions, it is critical that you capitalise on the feeling of motivation that you have by taking action. In many ways, it doesn't matter what action, as your own problem solving ability will generate a course of action for you once you are free of the problem. This first step will make sense to you and will be successful, if you can allow yourself to follow your instinct.

In any case, it's pointless writing a full action plan when your thinking is constrained by the problem. Do it only when you are feeling positive about the solution.

Too many people fail at this stage because they start planning instead of doing. They place too much emphasis on doing the right thing, rather than on doing something. Being able to do the right thing requires that you see into the future. Only time will reveal your success. The 'right thing' is only what you notice with hindsight. Take action now, any action.

When you have carried on taking action, noticing the results you get and using that information to generate new action, you will find, sooner or later, that you can now look back and write that specific, laborious action plan that you thought you needed.

History books are written by the victors. The same thing goes for business plans, CVs and your own autobiography.

Where?

It is important to know if the problem is universal (it happens everywhere) or if it is constrained to a particular place or context. This separates externally triggered problems from those that are caused by internal perception or beliefs.

Remember too that the problem isn't the problem; it's an example of it. You'll find the real problem lurking somewhere else.

One of the great contributors to the success of many management consultancies is the tendency to try to solve the wrong problem. Frequently, what looks like a problem is in fact merely a symptom. In order to get the most out of your problem solving resources, the first, the simplest and the most overlooked step is to find out where the problem is.

Whilst we often talk about companies, procedures, business processes and customer relationships as if they really exist, the fact is that these abstract components of business life are simply figments of the imaginations of real people like you. Business processes don't exist. A group of people doing the same kinds of activity in a particular sequence do exist. Therefore, it is important that you resist the temptation to conclude that you need a new business process in response to a problem. Business processes do not exist and my advice is never, ever create a business process. If you need to document what people do then watch some people doing the thing you need to document.

Recently, I had a conversation with someone about business processes in relation to knowledge and experience. In one aspect of an IT engineer's job, there is a twelve step process that defines how to connect an electrical cable. My friend said that he watched an experienced engineer prepare the cable and noticed that he only performed nine out of the twelve steps that were called for in the process. This proved that experienced people don't follow documented processes.

Part of the process required stripping the insulation off the cable, and the steps in the process were something like:

1. Measure 25mm from the end of the cable

2. Mark the cable at the 25mm point

3. Remove 25mm of the outer insulation

What my friend noticed was that the engineer didn't perform these steps, he just went ahead and stripped the insulation from the cable. I asked if the engineer had really skipped three of the steps, or if it only looked that way to a casual observer.

It turned out that the engineer had followed all twelve steps, but that something very important had happened for three of them.

He had done them in his head.

You can probably do it too. Hold up your finger and imagine a line that is 25mm or one inch from the fingertip. Now get a ruler and see how close you are.

For business processes and for problem solving, this is very, very important indeed. When people do things in their heads, business processes happen very quickly and very efficiently. On the other hand, people who write process documents hate this because it doesn't seem right. There is a very simple reason for this. The people who write the processes are asking the wrong questions. They are watching what appears to happen instead of noticing what really happens.

Specifically, they ask "why" too often, yet fail to ask the most important question of all - "how do you know?"

So, what appears to be happening on the surface is not usually the most important information you need to solve a problem. In particular, superficial information can guide you to the symptom of a problem rather than to its source.

And remember, "why?" doesn't get reasons, it gets reasoning. "How do you know?" gets real time decision making.

Imagine for a moment that processes and procedures do not exist. They only appear to exist because we notice patterns in the way that people excel in performing their jobs.

When people are performing their jobs well, they will be using various sources of information in order to make decisions. As far as each individual is concerned, that information comes from one of two places; inside their heads or outside of their heads. There, I told you this was easy.

When you are studying how someone does something, you will notice that there are certain points where they make a decision. Here is an illustration of this idea:

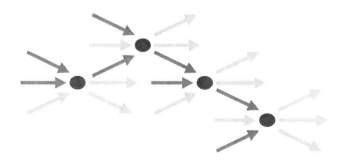

So, at each decision point, some information is considered and some is disregarded. One option is chosen above any others that may exist. How does this process take place? The person is doing something very complex and very important inside their head and it's that decision process that we need to investigate.

If you ask "how did you know how to do that" and the answer is internal, such as "I just know" or "from experience" or "I remember xyz" then the person is telling you that they have all the information they need to make that particular decision.

If they say something like "Fred told me" or "I read it from the manual" or "I measured it" then they are telling you that they are unable to make that decision without an external trigger. That trigger may be information or it may be permission - it makes no difference. What is important is that you are building a map of the human network that is operating.

As you begin to map out the process as it flows through a network of interconnected human brains, you will notice some strange things happening. Firstly, you may well find that there are loops. Secondly, you may find dead ends. Lastly, you may find that the people who actually do the things that are important sit at particular points in the network. As you stand back and take a fresh look at the map you have created, you may notice that the process is not a simple, straight line. Resist the temptation to make it one. Remember, you don't need to streamline or improve this process map as it is just a map - not the real world. Changing the map will not change the way that people think or make decisions. Streamlining the process so that it's easier for you to handle will not change the way that it operates in real life. In fact, if people have to learn your new process, you are actually making life harder for them.

A few years ago, we lived in a house on a new estate. Our next door neighbours weren't terribly pleasant people, and they applied for planning application to build an extension that would technically be within their boundaries but which would block the view from the front of our house as the houses were built at an angle to the road. We went along to the local council offices to find out how to object to their application.

In the council offices, there were lots of leaflets about how to apply for planning permission, and no information on how to object. You have to remember that the planning process is set up to give people permission. It presupposes that somebody wants to build something, but we can't have people building stuff willy-nilly, so we need a process to check applications before granting them. The process presupposes success.

So, we asked to meet a planning officer and once we had his full attention we asked him to teach us how the process works so that we could understand where the points of influence are.

There's no point just getting all upset, or shouting at the neighbours, or writing to the local newspaper, or complaining to your MP. These are not decision points in the process.

You've no doubt seen people complaining to someone who can't do anything to help. If you're going to complain, find the right person to complain to.

If you've ever travelled on the London Underground, you will have experienced first hand the effect of maps which are useful only when used in the context of a particular outcome. When you plan a route, you might look for the shortest or quickest journey, only to find that what looks like a simple connection is actually a ten minute walk. Conversely, you spend time trying to find a route between two stations, only to find that it would have been a two minute walk. Neither the tube map nor the street map are "accurate", so you use them both to guide your journey, not to dictate it.

If I were to make a generalisation about business processes and procedures, it would be this:

Bad procedures are written from a remote, dark cave and represent what you think ought to happen. Good procedures are created by learning what people do when they excel at their jobs and writing it down in a way that allows other people to copy it.

Learning what people do doesn't just mean watching them, and it certainly doesn't mean guessing what they are thinking. It means applying a set of exploratory linguistic tools to learn how they know what they know, and how they use that knowledge to decide on a course of action.

Bad procedures are like the scientific research books you find in University libraries. They exist and they are very likely to be true, but nobody reads them because they aren't useful - they don't mean anything. There is no possibility to adapt this information to the audience because it is the result of "objective" research and is therefore "true".

Good procedures are like fairy stories. Everyone knows them, everyone can learn easily from them and everyone enjoys passing them on to new generations. They are not strict rules which require uniformity - they are guidelines that generate excellence in those who believe in them. There is room for each individual storyteller to adapt the story to their own style without changing the essential information.

With a good procedure, we get predictable, uniform results even when the detailed procedural steps change.

Mapping procedures is a great way to find out where the problem lies. Mapping a procedure that isn't working or that has a problem is just as useful as mapping a good procedure, because whether a procedure is working or not doesn't matter. What matters is that you are mapping what is really happening. You don't need to have in mind the 'perfect' procedure which you intend to impose on the people in the organisation. Take what is happening now and prune out the loops and dead ends. You will find that the human network itself creates a new, optimal procedure.

You can apply this same set of principles to your own problems, or to other people. Mapping out a problem with genuine curiosity will get very different results than trying to fix it or offering advice. Mapping out the problem presumes that the person is working and that something useful is taking place. Let's take a problem that someone might have in a relationship. Let's not focus on what is wrong, what they are unhappy about and what the other person should be doing. If you remember, this is all irrelevant information because we can't change it.

If we map out the communication flows in the relationship, we find out what really happens. Now, in some context things will be good and in others it will be bad. For example, there are times when someone doesn't give you the attention you need, and others when they won't give you space for yourself. The pattern of behaviour is the same – their presence or absence does not coincide with your need for company. Are they are mind reader? Or is it better to tell them what you need from them? You will only notice a pattern like this if you find out what is happening in the relationship now and forget trying to find out what is right or wrong.

Another example – fear of public speaking, or fear or flying are quite complex problems in that the person with the fear has to do a lot of work to create the fear. By mapping out what happens, we can understand more about the problem. We can gain some remarkable insights simply by treating the problem as if it is a wonderful skill, to be studied and respected.

Someone I worked with was scared of flying, even though rationally he knew there was no need for it. Incidentally, this is another reason why talking about the problem doesn't help. The person already knows what they need to do about the problem, they just can't seem to find a way to do it.

So, I asked him all the questions you're familiar with by now. How did he know he was scared, how he knew it was time to get scared and so on. Something very interesting transpired. He was more scared on night flights and when flying business class. The one time he wasn't scared at all was when he got to sit in the cockpit and chat with the pilots during the flight (this was a few years ago). Interesting! It turned out that he ran through a very specific set of steps in preparing to scare himself. Firstly, if there were enough happy looking people around him, he would be happy. If the number of happy looking people dropped below a certain number, he would no longer have a basis for knowing to feel safe and he would imagine the ground crew doing pre-flight checks and missing out important things, forgetting to tighten bolts, forgetting to put important bits back and so on.

So in business class, there are fewer passengers around him for him to get his behavioural cues from. At night, everyone is asleep so they wouldn't know if the plane is going to crash or not. When he flew in the cockpit, he found that there were hundreds of dials and controls that he didn't understand, yet the pilots were chatting, having lunch and reading newspapers so obviously there was nothing to worry about. That's basically what the whole problem boiled down to – having enough people around, telling him not to worry means that he doesn't worry. Not enough people means he does worry. How do they tell him not to worry? By looking relaxed.

Now that we have mapped the problem out, impartially and respectfully, you can immediately see many ways to change it. You could change the number of people he needs to see, so we don't even have to change the problem, we just stop in from running in normal situations. You could change the implied 'don't worry' signal to an explicit one, so he could ask one of the cabin crew if everything is OK. You could even get him to imagine the ground crew doing their checks really diligently and carefully.

The most important aspect of this approach takes us back to the knowledge that this is an irrational fear. What we have done is to raise the complex, unconscious process into the person's awareness. They now know exactly how they make this a problem, and they can choose to do something differently. This means that you don't have to find the solution, you only have to break the problem.

You have no way of knowing, right now, what the "right" thing to do is because there is no single solution to a complex problem. You can take many different approaches to any problem and you may find that some work better than others. You must resist the temptation to conclude that this approach is the "right" one to use every time. All you know for certain is that it worked this time, on this problem. How do you know that it worked in isolation, and not as a consequence of you previously having tried a different approach that you had declared a failure? It's not only the last brick that makes a skyscraper the tallest building in the world.

Try everything and notice what works for you. As a problem solver, perhaps the most important thing is that you maintain a positive emotional state throughout. Declaring some of your abilities as "not working" will reduce your repertoire of skills and so the most powerful problem solvers are those who constantly extend their repertoire by being prepared to try anything in order to create a good outcome.

When you want to plan a long road journey, do you already know the perfect route before you open the map? If you do, then you will be very disappointed to learn that Motorways do not exist where you would like them to be, and the effort required to put them there is considerable. Instead, you look at the map to see what is already there. You know where you are now, and you know where you need to be, and by when.

You also have an idea of the type of journey you want - fast, quiet, scenic etc. Now, you overlay those broad requirements onto the map and your route creates itself as a mixture of supply and demand.

You can use the same basic principle when you want to optimise or create business processes. Start with the current location and destination. Overlay these onto the map that you have created. Finally, decide what kind of journey you would like. Now, watch as the route unfolds before your eyes.

When you are solving problems, it doesn't always matter where the problem is. Having an accurate map is the first step. Knowing where you are and where you want to be is the second step. The route, or solution, will appear before you, if you are open minded enough.

You can bear something else in mind when you're looking for solutions, which is that in order to solve a problem creatively, you don't have to find a solution – you just have to break the problem and allow the solution to emerge by itself.

In order to do this, you need an intention and that intention sets a direction. For example, if you sit down to help someone come up with a business plan, you would probably expect to have a business plan as a result of that conversation. Your intended outcome sets a direction; it is the outcome or destination on your map. Once you have established that, all you need to do is to create contrast, so that the person notices that they're not where they want to be. Generally, the greater the contrast, the greater the motivation to take action.

You could just create contrast in itself by shaking things up, but without an intention to provide a direction, the outcome will be random and disruptive. So begin with your intention, allow that to set a direction relative to where you are now and then give things a shake and notice what new ideas naturally emerge. Those ideas will only become solutions once you have put them into practice and found that they give you what you wanted.

We overturned the planning application. Amazingly, the application was technically acceptable, and we had no real reason to object as far as boundaries or planning guidelines were concerned. All that we did was to find out how to influence the process and then apply all of our energy in the most important places and with the most important people.

As E. Joseph Crossman said, "Obstacles are things a person sees when he takes his eyes off his goal."

Who?

We often assume that everyone thinks the same way as we do, yet this is rarely the case. You have experienced only your own thoughts for your entire life, so it can be difficult to understand how other people can perceive the world differently. If you can understand this then you will be very successful in solving interpersonal problems. If you have difficulty imagining how other people think differently to you, then at least accept that they do and accommodate these differences.

Asking who has the problem can be useful in separating people who can effect change from innocent bystanders. Remember too that the people with the problem are not necessarily the people with the resources to solve it.

It is always important to focus attention on the desired outcome rather than the problem so a useful "who" question to ask is "who has the resources to solve this problem?"

Attention is then neatly focussed on the acquisition of resources rather than on the problem itself. Certainly, if you are motivating a team of people involved in the problem, you will achieve far more useful results by guiding them forwards towards resources rather than backwards towards the source of the problem.

Wallowing in the problem is of absolutely no value whatsoever. If you cannot solve it and leave it behind, find someone who can.

Are you using your time and energy effectively? As a rule of thumb, you should devote your time and energy to issues which you can directly control or influence. Of course, it's obvious when you say it, yet we all seem to go round in circles at times, expending time and energy worrying about things that we can't change.

Often, people get very wrapped in other people's problems. For example, if your boss seems to be constantly trying to undermine you and stop you getting promoted, you can spend a lot of time trying to do things to change your boss's mind. Ultimately, your boss has a particular agenda and view of the world that you do not share, so you will always be ineffective at changing anyone's mind but your own.

Concentrate on what you can personally control. Who else will influence your promotion? Who else needs to be aware of your boss's behaviour? If you have problems that you are not in control of, give them to someone who can have a positive and direct influence. In other words, distribute the components of your problem to the people most able to effect change.

Here's a handy tool that you can use to help focus your attention on what you can personally achieve. This will help you to maximise the return on your own effort and make the best use of other people and resources.

Take two pieces of paper, and write a title on each one, like this:

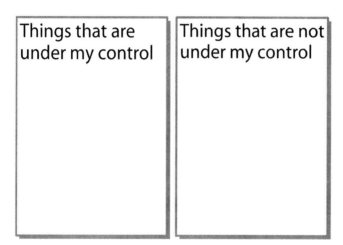

Make as long a list as you can on each piece of paper. In this exercise, "thing" means "an element or part of the problem".

Make sure that you include everything that is on your mind in relation to this problem. Take a few moments to review the lists and imagine how each of the items manifests itself. Make the two lists as real and compelling as you can. You might even begin to feel a little frustration at this point.

Next, tear up, screw up, burn or destroy in whatever way takes your fancy the sheet titled "Things that are not under my control".

Things that are
under my control

Now, just sit back and relax.

You don't need to do anything else at this point - just let your brain rearrange the problem for you. In the near future you will start finding ways to make the changes you desire because all your energy and time is now focussed on what you can do to directly influence events.

Strictly speaking, if you don't have direct control over an issue then it's not your issue. Get rid of it if you can, otherwise just forget about it.

Of course, you're quite right in thinking that you could just go through each item on your list and ask yourself "who is the right person to deal with this?" and that would be an excellent approach if you always thought as clearly as you are right now. When a problem is all around you, your view of the world becomes distorted and you no longer have access to the experience and mental agility that you take for granted at this moment.

All of these exercises are designed to distance you from the problem, giving you access to your own natural problem solving ability. This is why it isn't always important to start solving the problem consciously. It is only important to unpick the threads of the problem. Once you have conscious access to all of your natural skills, your brain will do the rest of the work for you.

This book will not give you the answers you seek on a plate. It will help you to break out of the problems that constrain your thinking, because questions are nearly always more useful than answers.

When?

Time is a great healer. Certainly, difficult situations that you may have experienced in the past seem less of a problem as you move further away from them. What is it about time that leads to this change in perception? Is it simply the passage of time, or did something specific happen during that time?

Problems don't just sort themselves out in the past - they can be solved in the future too. Can you imagine a time that you'll have solved this problem? In order to imagine this, you have to set aside the problem and pretend, for a moment, that it has already been solved. That alone makes quite a significant difference.

Does imagining that a problem has been solved actually solve the problem? Of course not! That's just ridiculous. The issue here is your capability to solve the problem. If you believe that you cannot solve a problem then your repertoire of behaviour and expertise will be greatly constrained. If you know that a problem has a solution that you have not found yet, then you will have access to a greater range of your own talents and experience.

Of course, if the problem only exists in your mind, and it's something to do with making a decision or finding an answer then perhaps you *can* solve the problem just by thinking differently.

The passage of time makes a huge difference to problems. Interior designers use many different methods to artificially age furniture, wood, metals and other materials to give them an antique look. Time could do the same thing, but the designers don't have the time to wait. The companies that manufacture the ageing kits didn't just resign themselves reluctantly to the fact that "time" ages materials - they asked, "what happens to the materials as time passes?"

Let's apply the same line of thought to our situation. What happens to problems as time passes? Remember that time is not the active agent - it is just the measurement of change in the world. Time is an illusion, a shared hallucination that convinces us that we need to wait for things to happen in due course, in their own time or even "all in good time". Well, we don't have the time to wait either, so let's see what happens to a problem with the passage of time.

Physicists know that time and space are closely connected and are in some situations interchangeable. If you put space between yourself and a problem, you get a fresh perspective, breathing space, room to move and a change that is as good as a rest. It turns out that the distance created by the passage of time has exactly the same effect.

You can create space just by walking away from the problem. You can create time in one of two ways - wait, or use your imagination. "But surely", you ask, "just imagining the passage of time doesn't make it real, therefore this is nonsense"

Well, don't knock it until you've tried it. If you've ever reminisced with friends about a memory that had a strong emotional content, then you know how easy it is to find yourself right back in that situation as if it were happening all over again.

Is there something special about the way that you recall memories that can make them so realistic? Yes, and the answer lies in your senses. The parts of your brain that process sensory information don't care whether that information comes from your external sensory organs or from your memory, so the memory seems real because it is real - the sensory input is happening to you right now but it's happening inside your mind. The key difference between "real life" and vivid imagination is that there are generally other people around to share "real life" experiences with, although there are many cases of groups of people sharing imaginations too.

Your brain is an analogue computer, so it doesn't have a way of reproducing zero or nothing - just like Roman numerals. In order to represent a different time or place, your brain creates a memory that is happening now. Even though the event took place a week ago, you are experiencing the memory right now. Otherwise, you would remember having had a memory. In general, people tend to relive old events in one of two ways - either as they experienced it or as if they are watching themselves in a film.

Think about a really emotionally charged memory, something really good and enjoyable - even exhilarating. As you think about it, allowing yourself to hear all the sounds and see all the sights, do you notice that the image is large, bright and clear? Do you notice that it's like being there, seeing everything through your own eyes?

Now think about an unhappy event that also has strong emotional connections for you. Maybe this is something that was embarrassing or stressful for you. Do you notice that the image is darker, less clear, maybe further away from you? You may already see yourself in this image, as if you are watching the scene from a bystander's point of view. If not, you may want to step out of the image, as if stepping out of a cinema screen. Walk some way off so that you can turn back and watch the whole scene from a neutral position, seeing yourself and your reactions from a distance.

Just before we move on, think about something that always makes you smile - even giggle. You should always leave people smiling.

Remember that everyone codes experience in their own way, so you will notice many differences between the ways that people represent emotional content. What we do know is that everyone has a way of coding the emotional content of memories, and it is connected to the structure of the memory. For example, two memories with the same emotional attachment would both have pictures that were directly ahead, above eye level, bright, colourful and with a border like a photo. The content of the photo is specific to the memory. The structure of the photo is specific to the emotional attachment.

In the first example that you thought of, watching the experience through your own eyes is known as being "associated". In the second example, watching the experience as a bystander is known as being "dissociated". The interesting thing about these two points of view is the way that the emotional content works.

Let's say that you had an experience in the past that makes you feel tense in your stomach every time you think about it, almost to the point of feeling sick. Maybe, in ten years time, you'll be able to think about the experience without that feeling and learn something useful from it. What would be good right now would be to think about the experience without the emotional response, learn what's useful and consign the rest to history. This will allow you to learn any valuable lessons and then get on with your life.

The basic technique here is to imagine distancing yourself from the experience and you can do this using either space or time. Here are a few tools you can use to help you do this. All you need to make them work for you is a little imagination.

To use each of these techniques, all you need is a specific memory to work with and somewhere that you won't be distracted for a few minutes. Some people can easily do this in a crowded bar or on a train, others need complete silence. Just go with whatever works for you. You may also find it's easier to lead someone else through the process than to do it yourself as your attention can be completely on either the process or the content - not both. Therefore, you may want to get someone else to read the instructions to you, at least for the first time you do it. In any case, have a read through the techniques first and begin to imagine how they might work before you try them out for real.

Fast forward

Just watch the whole scene unfold as you run through the memory, as if you're watching a film. As you reach the end of the experience, pause the film so that the action is frozen. Look around and notice whatever seems important.

Now, run the film backwards, rewinding it quickly and seeing the action in reverse. If it helps, you can imagine the projectionist pressing buttons up in the control room. Run the film backwards right back to the start of this scene. Now pause again and run the film forwards at double speed. Notice how funny people's movements look and how their voices are high pitched. Now that you have control over the film, run it backwards and forwards as many times as you like. Finally, let it run through from start to finish at normal speed and notice how your emotional response has changed.

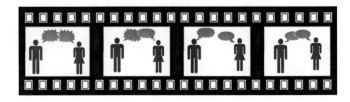

At the cinema

Just watch the whole scene unfold as you run through the memory like watching a film. Keep looping the whole scene over and over.

As you let the film run, imagine you can step out of your body and step out through the screen into a cinema. Go and find an empty seat and sit down.

Now look back up at the screen and watch the scene as it continues to run. See the flickering of the projector and the other seats around you. If you still have any emotional response to what you see, take another step backwards out of your body and go and sit at the back of the cinema.

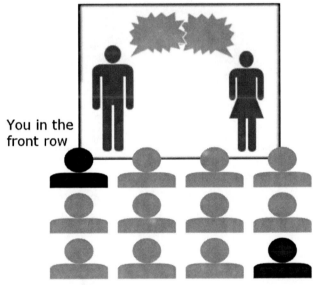

You in the front row

You in the back row

Watch the back of your head and notice how you look as you watch the film on the screen. Watch yourself, watching yourself on screen. This sounds odd, so give it a go and find out how easy it is to imagine an experience this way.

Watch the film as it runs from start to end and then rewind it back to the start, seeing the action move quickly in reverse, just like when you press 'rewind' on your video recorder at home. Watch the whole film again at double speed, then rewind it. Keep running the whole film forwards and backwards until the emotional response has gone completely.

Walk back to the projector screen, then step through it into the action. Step back into yourself and continue running the film, noticing how your emotional response has changed.

A new perspective

Another variation of this exercise is very useful for dealing with past problems that involve relationships of some kind. The problem may be as simple as a conversation or meeting that went badly right up to a fear of public speaking. It's a really nice, simple exercise that you can easily run through yourself, or lead someone else through, conversationally.

Let's take a really common problem - a fear of presenting in front of an audience, or a belief that you are "bad" at presenting. First, remember a specific time that you presented and felt it went badly for you. If you have developed your current perception since a specific experience, it's a good idea to work with that experience.

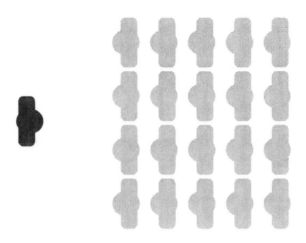

Imagine watching a film of the presentation, viewed through your own eyes looking out to the audience, starting just before it starts to go badly and ending just afterwards. Recall the experience in as much detail as you can, making sure you have the sounds and feelings as well as what you saw.

Step two is to remember what you had for breakfast, and what you heard as you woke up this morning.

It's important with all these exercises to change your focus of attention between steps.

The real step two is to imagine yourself walking into the presentation room and sitting down as a member of the audience. Take a moment to look around you and see the other audience members.

Look to the front of the room and see yourself presenting. Watch and listen as you see yourself deliver the presentation and run a short film through from this new viewpoint. Pay attention to anything you notice at the point you thought it had "gone wrong".

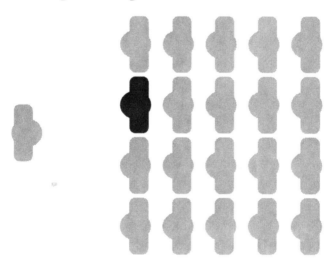

What do you remember about your first car? What were the seats made of?

Step three is to imagine yourself walking past the presentation room and stopping to peer in through the window.

You can see both yourself presenting and yourself in the audience, and as you look from one to the other, you can see how they relate to each other. As you watch, hearing only muffled sounds, you can run the movie of the presentation again, and notice anything that you want to notice about it.

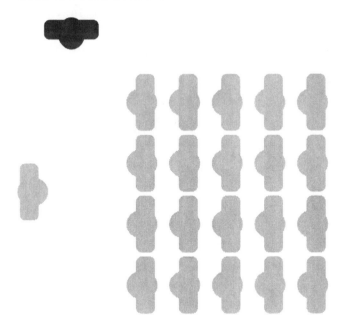

What was your favourite toy as a child? Did it make a sound?

Now, bring what you've learned from these two new viewpoints back with you as you return to your starting point, delivering the presentation. Run the movie again, and this time pay close attention to how your feelings and perceptions have changed as a result of this new information. Use this new perception to rehearse the next presentation you will deliver, quickly in your mind. Above all, enjoy the realisation that learning from your mistakes is something you can do in complete privacy!

The confusion technique

Sometimes, old memories just need a bit of jumbling up. The results you got in the past only become "the results you always get" when you decide to make things turn out that way. People often say, "I always do that" when what they really mean is "I used to do that, and I confuse the past with the choices I make now".

If you believe that patterns of behaviour and results in the past extend into the future so that you "always" achieve a certain outcome, here's a good exercise for you.

First, imagine a strip of film on a table in front of you. Look carefully at the frames and see how they represent the progress of a particular situation that you would like to be different, from the first time it happened to the last time. Now, put that film strip into a projector and watch a film of the progress and development of this situation.

Now, choose an area of your life where things have developed and progressed very nicely. It may be your career, your love life, your children or your changing hairstyles over the years. Imagine another strip of film that shows the progress of this area and run it through the projector, watching the film as it progresses from the start to where you are now.

Both film strips should be the same length.

Now, put both pieces of film on the table. Look at them both lying side by side.

Pick up the "good" film strip and place it on top of the "problem" film strip.

Pick them both up together and place them into the projector. Get some tape and join the ends together, so that the films run in a continuous loop, then keep on watching the two films together. At first, it might be hard to keep running through the jumble of images, that's why you've joined it into a loop so that you can let it run over and over again until it becomes easy.

Now, take the film out of the projector and undo the tape that joins the ends together. Add a new, blank piece of film onto the end of the sequence.

And now run the whole sequence through again, this time extending the sequence into the future by creating new frames as the film plays - new frames that contain the progress you'll make and the success you'll achieve, having completely resolved this situation and with the resources to achieve more than your wildest dreams.

Finally, run the whole new sequence through a few times until it becomes easy to imagine yourself having solved your old problems, moving on and achieving everything you could hope for.

Time travel

Imagine a line that represents the flow of time. It may go from front to back, side to side or even up to down. Whatever comes naturally to mind is right for you.

Imagine yourself standing on this line at a point that represents "now". If you like, you can physically walk up and down for this exercise - some people find it easier to imagine it that way.

See your problem on the line, pay attention to where it is. Walk up to the problem and take a look at it. Now walk to a point on the line that lies just past the problem, just in the future from it. Look back at the problem from a point when it has just recently been solved. Notice anything that you think is important as you look at the back of the problem.

Now, walk to a time in the future that lies way beyond the problem, when it's a distant memory. Look back at the problem and, if you can still see it, notice anything that you think is important.

Next, walk to a point that's many years ahead. Turn round and look back at the problem as a tiny speck off in the distance. Notice all the things you've achieved in your life since solving that problem, and allow yourself to feel good about those achievements.

Finally, walk back to the present moment, collecting up and taking with you anything important that will be of use to you today. When you arrive back at the present moment, look at the problem again and notice anything that has changed.

Home movies

For this exercise, you can imagine yourself sitting in the editing room of a film studio.

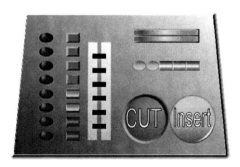

You're in front of a mixing desk and there are rolls of film and audio tape on a shelf above you. You watch the film run through on the screen as before, but this time you're able to control the editing machine so that you can run the film forwards, backwards or at any speed. You're looking for a specific point in the memory where you really start to feel the emotional attachment.

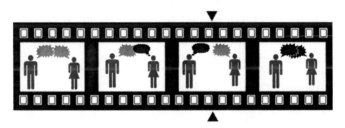

You're slowly moving the film backwards and forwards until you find the exact point at which you start to have the response that you want to change. Press the big red "cut" button on the mixing desk to cut the tape at that point.

Now you can fast forward until well after the event, to a time when your emotional state had returned to normal. Press that big red button again. The part of the film that has the unwanted emotional response has now been removed. Your next job is to put in a new piece of film.

Have a look through the rolls of film on the shelf until you find one marked with the kind of emotional response that would have been more useful to you at the time. When you find one you like, take out the film and feed it into the editing machine. Press the big green "Insert" button and now run the film through again, watching how different it looks with the new response.

You'll notice that the response doesn't have to be perfect - only different to what happened last time. If you like, you can try a number of different responses and see which works best. Often, the response that achieves the best outcome for you is one that you wouldn't have thought about.

There's nothing to be gained in letting problems survive for longer than they need to. Deal with them, and then get on with your life.

Which?

As a 'thank you' for reading this far, you get a special bonus question! It's like having a bonus level in a computer game to reward you for shooting all the aliens.

People often get stuck in dilemmas. They have no trouble moving forwards or being motivated to take action, they just don't know which action to take. They're paralysed by choice, and when they can't imagine which choice will turn out for the best, they go round in circles.

People do not stay still. No situation is completely static or stuck - in this book I've already talked about people being stuck and in the next chapter you'll learn about the famous Unsticker. In fact, people aren't immobilised; they just don't seem to be moving if you watch them over long periods of time.

Here's a picture of 'stuckness'. This person is resting up against the obstacle, unable to move. Like a piece in a game of draughts, the person can only move forwards and when they reach an obstacle, they get stuck.

Of course, real people are usually able to move in different directions. For an obstacle that someone overcomes easily, they go around or over it. When you find there's no milk in the fridge at home, it's no big deal - you go and buy some more. When there's no milk in the fridge at work, it's a big deal, it's someone else's fault for taking all the milk and being so selfish.

If we look at this situation objectively, there's just no milk. That's it. It's only the meaning that we place on it that makes it a problem. What makes it a stuck problem is the way that the person is unable to take any action to resolve it or move past it.

So, let's see a picture of what is more likely to happen in a "stuck" situation:

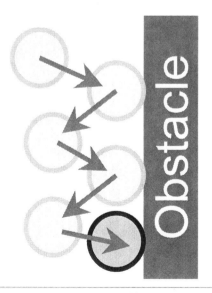

You can see what's happening here - the person is moving backwards and forwards, always trying to move but being constrained by the problem. They can move in any direction except forwards because that's where the obstacle is.

People in this situation appear to be very busy, and they're always doing something, it's just not helping them.

There's one more scenario to consider:

Here's a person who rotates between the obstacle and a previous, more comfortable situation. They are literally going round in circles. In the above example, the person has choice but they don't know how to get past the obstacle. In this example, the person has no choice - they can either do what they used to do or try to do what they want to do. They can only occupy two positions and they just spin aimlessly.

So, what about dilemmas? A dilemma is an interesting type of problem in that there's no obstacle involved other than making the choice itself. When people have many choices, there's lots of information available that helps them to make a decision. When someone only has two choices, there's not enough information to choose one over the other. A choice only becomes a dilemma when there's insufficient difference between the choices. You, as an objective bystander can see lots of differences but it's important that you remember this: the differences you can see are not important ones. They are not part of the person's decision criteria, therefore they won't help.

Here's a picture of a dilemma:

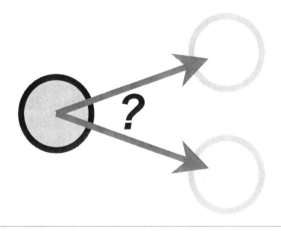

You can see right away that there are some interesting beliefs that generate a dilemma - and you might think of some more:

□   There are only two choices

□   A choice must be made

□   To choose means to change or move

□   The choices are mutually exclusive

Now, if you really believed that you could only have one thing or the other, not both, and that your choice is limited to what you have in front of you then you can easily imagine how difficult you would make your life.

Did you catch that? How difficult *you* would make your life - it's your choice entirely!

You solve dilemmas like this all day, every day, simply as a result of having more useful beliefs about your choices. For example, do you drive to work or take the bus? That's a dilemma. Do you drive to work or have pizza for lunch. Not a dilemma. Do you see why? In the second example, the choices are not mutually exclusive. They're not choices, so you don't create a dilemma for yourself. The first example probably wasn't a dilemma either, it could have been a 'no brainer' because it wasn't really a choice at all. You can have it all!

Do you ever sit and ponder over what you're going to order at an all you can eat buffet restaurant? You can have it all! Compare that to the angst that people go through as they sit examining a menu – "if I have the beef I can have red wine but the chicken looks nice but then I couldn't have red wine and I quite fancy red wine tonight".

So the logical chain of thought goes:

Red wine > Beef > Chicken > Red wine

And you go round and round in circles until the waiter comes over and you are forced to make a decision which you then sit and think about until you actually get your meal and start eating, because at the point at which the waiter takes your order, you still haven't made a decision. You order based on whichever point you're at in the loop, but you have not really reached a decision. In sales, this is called 'buyer's remorse' and it's worth bearing in mind that people do not change their minds – they just carry on processing a decision that they have not yet made. We don't change our minds because we are remarkably consistent creatures. Inconsistency or indecision is an illusion – the reality is that we force people to put choices into words that have not yet been made.

The problem is rules – rules that constrain our choices. As Morpheus said, "some rules can be bent, others broken."

So, being in a dilemma is as good as being stuck. What good things can we say about dilemmas? Well, being in a dilemma means:

- You have choice
- You want to move or change
- You know roughly what you want

So, I will give you the following useful belief about a dilemma:

Being in a dilemma does not mean you can't choose. It means that you don't know *how* to choose.

Now, building a method for choosing is much easier than making a choice. Of course, once you have a method or process, the choice is made for you.

Here are some questions that you might find helpful in resolving a dilemma.

What is it about the options that makes this a dilemma? What is the single element of the options that means it's impossible to rate one higher than the other? Discard all the stuff that's different but unimportant. Keep to what's important. Focus on why these are choices in the first place. For example, let's say you can't decide on car A or car B. Why isn't bicycle C a choice? It's the right colour, it's easy to park and the insurance will be low, yet it's not a choice. So, what is important about the choices you have?

If I took away choice A (or B) now, would you be happy with the result? In other words, is this a problem of choice or a problem of necessity? If someone else forces a dilemma on you, for example if you're a manager and your boss says "you must make either Jim or Fred redundant" then that might be a dilemma. If someone else makes the decision for you, is that helpful? Another way of doing this is to toss a coin and pay attention to whether you feel more or less relieved with the result.

If you could create choice C that had everything you want in it, what would it be like? So, is this a problem of limited choices? Perhaps you need to buy a new hat and you can't decide between red and green. If you knew they had blue in the stock room, the choice would be easy. It's only a dilemma because you believe your choices are limited.

What stops you from having both A and B? Some people create dilemmas by splitting options that are really just components of the same option. You can help them with this by moving up to a level of thinking that encompasses both A and B. For example, you can ask, "What's important about both of those options? What will either of them give you?"

Do you need to decide now? Is this an enforced dilemma, or does the choice even need to be made at all? In other words, if left alone, will the decision make itself? Is this a dilemma caused by a decision being made before its time? For example, you have a meeting at work to decide on a course of action. Five o'clock comes round and you're no closer to a decision, so the boss says "right - we have to make a decision before we go home". Why? If the decision isn't ready, and if it's important enough, sleep on it!

What do both A and B achieve for you? Once the decision is made, what happens next? Presumably, both choices achieve a similar outcome, so what is that outcome? When you've made your choice, what will you have?

Here's a metaphorical trick for you. You've probably seen these puzzles in magazines and children's books, where you have to trace the lines from start to finish and find out which start point leads to the end point:

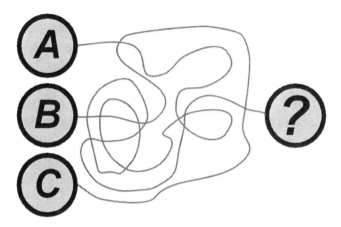

You can work within the rules imposed by the puzzle designer - that you start at the start and work by trial and error until you reach the end, or you can move outside of the rules of the game - starting at the end and working back to the start.

When you start at the start, you have many possible choices. When you start at the end, you have only one possible choice - the one that worked.

So, possibly the quickest way to deal with a dilemma is to move past the point of decision to the lasting outcome, then work backwards until you find out the decision. For a complex dilemma, it's a good idea to always work back from the outcome, even just as a way to explore the implications of making each choice in the future. The decision may be based only on information available now - extending the decision into the future can make the decision easier to make, as more information usually means better decisions.

For this, we can use an imaginary time line again. Imagine you are standing on a line that connects past, present and future, and that at some point in the future you can see the dilemma as a fork or branch in the timeline.

Walk into the future, and explore the first branch of the timeline, representing the first choice of action. Walk a long way in to the future and think about where this choice takes you, then walk back to the present.

Continue to explore all branches of the timeline, to get a sense of what each of these choices means, how the future will turn out and finally to what long term point all of these choices will take you. As you stand at the present moment, just allow all this new information to soak in. Now, step off the timeline and walk to the other end, where all of the branches converge at some point in the distant future. Even if these branches seem to take your life in totally different directions, you will find that they all converge at the end of your life. As you stand just past that convergence point, look back to the present and walk, intuitively, back to the present, noticing which branch you chose to follow back. Perhaps you even created some new choices for yourself that incorporated some of the aspects of the other choices to create something that gave you everything you wanted.

The world famous Unsticker

Being stuck can be a sign that you're just too close to the problem. It's easy to spend lots of time and effort trying to solve problems that you don't need. At times like this, a really effective way of getting unstuck is to have someone ask you a great question that sets you thinking again. Often, when you talk to someone about a problem, they ask you the "why" question which doesn't help.

How can you have someone ask you exactly the right kind of question? Well, when you look at the Change Magic website at www.changemagic.com, you'll find an online Unsticker that you can use yourself. Alternatively, you can use this list to unstick yourself, or you can give it to a friend or colleague and have them ask you questions. All you need to do is pick numbers randomly - shake some dice or use the time as a way of picking random questions. It's important that you don't go through the list, looking for the 'right' question, as that's not the point of the exercise. Often, the most oblique or unusual idea is the one that really starts you thinking. If you search for the 'right' question, you're just confirming the problem.

At the end of the list, there's an explanation of how the questions work, if you're interested.

It's very important that you choose questions randomly rather than looking through the list and picking a 'good' question. Picking a 'good' question means you've found one that fits inside the problem, so it won't help you. You could use digits from telephone numbers, throw darts or roll dice. You could just open a page and point at a question, or you could get a friend or colleague to call out random numbers.

Now, all you need to do is hold the problem clearly in your mind. Really think about what the problem means to you and how you describe it. Spend a few moments clarifying the problem, decision or question to make sure you clearly know what it is you're solving. It will make a difference if you get someone else to do the asking, or at least repeat the question using someone else's voice in your head.

Then just ask away!

1	Are you worrying about the right problem?
2	Do you remember that time you were really creative?
3	I'm not quite sure I understand. Can you think that from a different perspective?
4	How heavy is this problem?
5	Why don't you?
6	What won't you do?
7	When will you have solved this problem yet?
8	What's the one thing you would like most of all, right now?
9	Who can you trust?
10	What does this problem sound like?
11	How fast is this problem?
12	Shall we just go for a drink instead?
13	Imagine a close colleague has this problem. What is your advice to them?
14	Hmmmmmmmmmm....... That's interesting

15	What would happen if you simply forgot all about this, right now?
16	What colour is this problem?
17	If this problem was a bug, would you squash it or put it outside?
18	Which part of this problem is the most ticklish?
19	Do you secretly enjoy having this problem?
20	Was this a problem a month ago?
21	Can you think of a single good reason to keep this problem?
22	What have you done to earn this problem?
23	A travelling salesman throws this problem on the floor to demonstrate a new vacuum cleaner. Do you buy the vacuum cleaner?
24	Where would this problem be without you?
25	In years to come, will you be glad that you had this problem?
26	As you see yourself with this problem, what makes you smile?
27	What wouldn't happen if you didn't?

28	When you have solved this problem, what will you do with all that spare time?
29	What would be the worst question for me to ask you now?
30	What gives you the right to have this problem?
31	If the Change Magician could grant you one wish, what would it be?
32	Will you miss having this problem around?
33	When?
34	If this problem was a fruit, what fruit would it be?
35	Stop.... And think for just a moment
36	Who?
37	Who else knows about this?
38	Imagine you bought a new pair of trousers and found this problem in the pocket. Would you tell the shopkeeper?
39	If this problem went away right now, what would you do with all that free time?
40	Why not sleep on it?
41	How light is this problem?

42	What kind of animal could solve this problem?
43	How will having had this problem have helped you?
44	Think of someone you know who you hate. What would they do?
45	Think of someone you know who you distrust. What would they do?
46	What shouldn't you do?
47	Was this a problem a week ago?
48	If you won this problem in a raffle, would you give it back?
49	Oooh...that's a good one...
50	Oh, that's good. Let me write it down...
51	How slow is this problem?
52	What does this problem prove?
53	After you've solved this problem, will you miss it?
54	What does this problem do for you?
55	If this problem was a shop, what shop would it be?

56	Is there something more important beneath this?
57	As you look back on this, which question made you smile the most?
58	Who else does this involve?
59	How could this problem benefit someone else?
60	Are you certain this is your problem?
61	What can you do?
62	What should you do?
63	As you see yourself with this problem, what strikes you as funny?
64	Do you need this problem?
65	What size is this problem?
66	How do you know that this is a problem for you?
67	How does this problem benefit you?
68	Who cares enough about you to help you?
69	Imagine I could wave a magic wand and make this problem go away, would you miss it?

70	If this problem was a vegetable, what vegetable would it be?
71	What would be the most useful question for me to ask you now?
72	How does this problem help you?
73	Why?
74	What can't you do?
75	If your child brought this problem home from school and said "look what I made!" would you pretend to like it?
76	If you found a wallet with this problem in it, would you hand it in to the police?
77	Are you secretly in love with this problem?
78	What would happen if you did?
79	As you see yourself with this problem, what strikes you as odd?
80	What did you do differently last time?
81	Imagine it's a week from now. How has the problem changed?
82	What do you want most of all?

83	If this problem was a piece of music, what music would it be?
84	Is this a problem that you need?
85	Is this problem really a symptom?
86	What if you were wrong about this?
87	How do you know?
88	If this problem was a musical instrument, what instrument would it be?
89	I want to make sure I understand...can you think that from someone else's point of view?
90	Was this a problem ten years ago?
91	What wouldn't you do?
92	How will having had this problem help you grow?
93	Think of someone you know who you love. What would they do?
94	What kind of glue could stick this problem?
95	What does this problem taste like?
96	What extra resource or skill would make the biggest difference to you, right now?

97	Who can you depend on?
98	Imagine your best friend has this problem. What is your advice to them?
99	Why are you?
100	What kind of cake could solve this problem?
101	So what?
102	What does this problem mean?
103	What will you do differently next time?
104	What do you want to happen?
105	Which part of this problem is the most spiky?
106	Imagine it's a year from now. How has the problem changed?
107	Who can you rely on?
108	What?
109	If you had a voodoo doll, who would you give this problem to?
110	Why bother?

111	Do you remember that time you laughed until you cried?
112	When did you first start to realise this?
113	Was this a problem a day ago?
114	If you found this problem in a cabbage would you complain?
115	What shape is this problem?
116	How will having had this problem have changed you?
117	After you've solved this problem, what will be the next one?
118	Imagine it's a day from now. How has the problem changed?
119	What does this problem symbolise?
120	What if this was really someone else's problem?
121	When you look back on this problem, what will make you laugh most?
122	Is someone up there trying to tell you something?
123	What will be the best thing about having had this problem?

124	How will having had this problem help you develop?
125	A travelling salesman tries to sell you this problem. Do you buy it?
126	Where?
127	Do you remember that time you got into so much trouble?
128	Imagine your parent has this problem. What is your advice to them?
129	Imagine it's a month from now. How has the problem changed?
130	As you see yourself with this problem, what strikes you as interesting?
131	As you look back on this, which question was the one that really helped you most?
132	If the fairies came and took this problem away, what would you spend the 10p on?
133	Think of someone you know who you trust. What would they do?
134	I want to make sure I understand you...what is it that you want to happen?
135	What would be the best question for me to ask you now?
136	What would happen if you didn't?

137	When do you want this to change?
138	As you see yourself with this problem, what strikes you as curious?
139	What if?
140	How?
141	What is this problem a sign of?
142	How is this a problem right now?
143	What mustn't you do?
144	What would be the most helpful question for me to ask you now?
145	What kind of car could run over this problem?
146	Think of someone you know who you respect. What would they do?
147	As you look back on this, which question was the hardest to answer?
148	When did you first find out about this?
149	Let me think about that one for a moment...
150	How do you know you're right?

151	What is this problem a symptom of?
152	Think of someone you know who you envy. What would they do?
153	What wouldn't you do?
154	What does this problem show?
155	What kind of rock could forget this problem?
156	What would happen if this just slipped your mind?
157	Do you need anyone else to do this for you?
158	After you've solved this problem, who will you celebrate with?
159	Who cares enough about the outcome of this to help you?
160	Who stands to gain if you solve this?
161	How does it feel to know you can laugh about this?
162	Imagine your child has this problem. What is your advice to them?
163	What wouldn't happen if you did?
164	Imagine your favourite school teacher has this problem. What is your advice to them?

165	What must you do?
166	How will having had this problem have improved you?
167	I want to make sure I understand you...what is it that you don't want to happen?
168	If this problem was a person, where would you hit him/her?
169	If you saw this problem in trouble, would you help it?
170	What will you do?
171	What has been the turning point for this problem?
172	Which part of this problem is the most furry?
173	What would you be doing now if things were different?
174	What does this problem demonstrate?
175	What would you do if things weren't the same?
176	As you see yourself with this problem, what do you notice first?
177	Was this a problem a year ago?
178	When did you last worry about this?

179	I'm not quite sure I understand. Can you think that a different way?
180	Imagine your favourite cartoon character has this problem. What is your advice to them?
181	What does this problem signify?
182	When did you last think about this?
183	When did you first start to think this way?
184	What needs to happen for this problem to disappear?
185	After you've solved this problem, what will you do next?
186	Who else is concerned about this?
187	If you came home from shopping and found that the shop hadn't charged you for this problem, would you own up?
188	What would you do?
189	As you see yourself with this problem, what strikes you as sad?
190	Imagine your favourite actor/actress has this problem. What is your advice to them?
191	What makes you so lucky that you could have a problem like this?

192	How could you make money out of this problem?
193	When did you first know about this?
194	What does this problem smell like?
195	How does this problem fade in the sunlight?
196	Who can you turn to?
197	Imagine it's ten years from now. How has the problem changed?
198	What temperature should you wash this problem at?
199	How shiny is this problem?
200	If this problem was a car, what car would it be?

About the questions

If you would like to know more about the questions, you can read this chapter. If you'd rather believe that they're just magic, don't read any further!

The questions are broadly split into the following categories, although some questions actually do several things for you at once.

Representation

Some questions attack the way that you represent the problem to yourself. When you are away from the problem - people, a place or whatever - you still carry it with you as a collection of memories. Those memories are arranged in a special, unique way that collectively forms "the problem". As the problem changes, the representation changes. Does the opposite happen too? Yes, if we play with the representation, the problem changes. When your brain notices that the problem can change it very quickly learns that the problem is under your control and this starts a process of reorganisation, during which you will have many creative insights that help you deal with the problem.

Resource

Generally, you have everything you need to deal with any problem you would ever face. At some point in the past, you have had an experience which is relevant to whatever situation you find yourself in now or in the future. What often happens in the case of 'problem thinking' is that this experience does not readily translate from one context of your life to another. For example, someone who has a job as a salesman may be unable to talk to strangers at parties. Can you imagine a salesman not being able to talk to strangers? "Aahh...that's different" he would say, and he is right - it is different. It's still relevant though, so what we need to do is get the skills to transfer - to get him to make connections from one area of his life to another. People who are very flexible and adaptable do this naturally. The resource questions help you to find relevant experience to deal with this problem, which may come from the past, the future or from other people. Remember that if you do 'what someone else would do' you are in fact using your own skills! This other person doesn't live in your head, so you use information from a different part of your brain to provide the answers you need. It was still in your head, it was just stored somewhere out of reach.

Dissociation

Being too close to a problem means that you can't see round or over it and you can't tell how big it is. When you take a break from something and go back to it, only to see it differently, you are dissociating yourself from the problem. When you go on holiday and come back with new ways of tackling old problems, you have dissociated yourself. When you think back to a problem you had ten years ago and laugh at yourself, you are now dissociated. Dissociation is a very powerful tool and is used in many situations including phobia cures and personal change. Here, dissociation questions are used to help you gain some distance from the problem. This might help you to see round it to the real goal, it might help you to get a sense of the size of the problem or it may just give you some breathing space.

Reframe

Reframing is what happens when you take something that you are totally certain about and add in a new piece of information that throws your certainty out of the window. Reframing attacks subjective meaning; in other words when you have a group of memories that you have collected together and summarised with a meaning, you have added information from your own experience that may or may not be useful.

For example, you might collect some experiences together at work and attach the meaning "I'm never going to get promoted here, they have their favourites and I'm not one of them". You have no way of knowing if that is true or not, but it becomes true because you believe it. To make matters worse, you then filter new experiences through this meaning. If you did get promoted, it would be because they felt sorry for you, or because no-one else was left, or because they wanted a scapegoat. What kind of manager would you be with this attitude? Reframing just picks at the loose threads of meaning, giving you a chance to build a new, more useful one.

State

If you're feeling miserable, it's probably not a good time to write a life plan. If you're feeling dejected, it's not a good time to go for a job interview. The weight of a problem can really affect your state and thereby your ability to deal with the problem. When you're feeling bright and bouncy, you just shrug things off that would seem like major problems if you were feeling down. Your state is another filter through which you interpret the world, so before you can find a solution to a problem you need to change your state from a 'problem state' to a 'solution state'. There are many ways to do this which mostly fall into two main categories - physiology and focus of attention. In other words you can go for some fresh air or think about something else for a while. The state questions divert your attention to something else. Some of them might be a little odd or even confusing and that's intentional as confusion is another way of changing how you think and therefore your state.

You'll notice that all of the questions therefore have a common theme, even though they work in different ways. The common theme is that they all change the way you think, changing your state and changing the framework of the problem.

You don't have to worry about solving a problem, you just have to give it a good shake and your brain will do the rest for you. That, in essence, is what creative problem solving is all about - not wasting time trying to find the *right* answer and instead realising that any and every answer is right - because it moves you away from the problem. Only with the benefit of hindsight - and with a little help from Six Questions - can you know which answer was right.

Now what?

Well, now that you have many new ways to solve those problems, you can start by getting rid of all those lingering, niggling problems that you don't need any more. When you've done that, you can start on other people's problems.

It's important to get some practice first before you go around trying to fix people. It's important that you understand the internal processes that go on inside you when you change the way that you think about something. It's vital that you learn for yourself the critical lesson when you're helping people solve problems. Just because someone's quiet doesn't mean they're not busy.

When you ask people questions, or suggest ideas to them that change the way they think, they often do odd things. They look up, and down, and sideways. They "hhmmm" and they "aahhh" and they'll eventually look right at you and say "you're right! That's a great idea!" You may be confused by this and think "I don't remember suggesting anything" and that's OK. Frequently, you will be there when people solve their problems and they will blame you for it. Accept it graciously.

Finally, bear this in mind. Not everyone wants to solve their problems. Problems come in very handy sometimes and some people will get upset if you try to take their comfort blankets away. Just tread carefully.

Well, thank you for reading and I hope that you'll keep this book handy as a problem solving resource. If I can be of any help, you can email me at **questions@ciauk.com** and don't forget to keep using the online resources at **www.changemagic.com**

Take care and have even more fun!

Further learning

NLP in Business

A practical handbook to help you apply NLP professionally – with special chapters on leadership, sales, coaching, teams and presenting.

ISBN 978-0-9545748-3-3

NLP - Skills for Learning

A practical handbook to help you apply NLP in learning, teaching, training and presenting.

ISBN 978-0-9545748-0-2

Change Magic

The evolutionary approach to organisational change.

ISBN 978-0-9545748-2-6

The Unsticker

376 new questions to get you unstuck in a handy new pocket format.

ISBN 978-0-9545748-4-0

Thank you

Liz, for helping me to make the space and time to do things like this.

My Dad, Phil, who showed me that anything is possible, and also that any problem can be solved with enough effort and swearing.

Brian Corrigan for reading the very first draft.

Steve Cordell for his feedback on the questions.

Harry, Karl, Jerome and David for encouraging me with such lovely reviews.

Andy Bradbury for promising not to savage this book in his review!

Michael Beale for his assertion that big thick books are bought because they look good on the shelf, whereas short books like this actually get read and used. He helped me see that this would be a worthwhile thing to do.

All the clients who, over the past 8 years, have shared their wonderful experiences with me.

And finally to you – for taking action (by buying this book) to live the way you want to live, free from problems and with your wildest dreams brought vividly to life.

Printed in the United Kingdom by
Lightning Source UK Ltd., Milton Keynes
139647UK00001B/20/P